D1573017

CHESTERFIELD COUNTY PUBLIC LIBRARY
CHESTERFIELD, VA

History of America

SLAVERY

A Chapter in American History

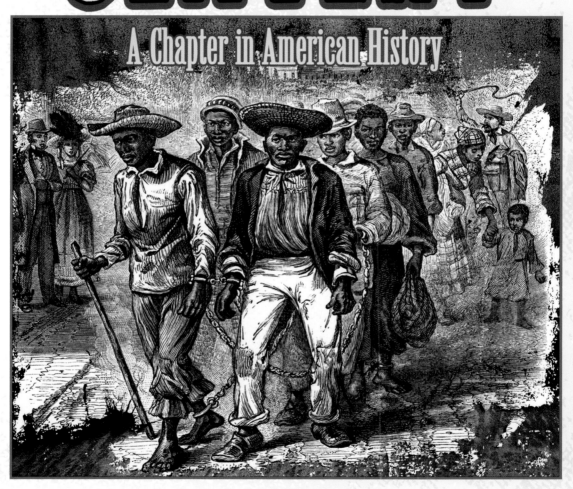

Written by **Katie Marsico**

Educational Media

rourkeeducationalmedia.com

Scan for Related Titles
and Teacher Resources

© 2014 Rourke Educational Media

All rights reserved. No part of this book may be reproduced or utilized in any form or by any means, electronic or mechanical including photocopying, recording, or by any information storage and retrieval system without permission in writing from the publisher.

www.rourkeeducationalmedia.com

Photo credits: American School/Getty Images, cover; Joy Rector/Shutterstock Images, cover, 5, 13, 19, 27, 35; North Wind Picture Archives/Photolibrary, 4, 6, 12, 14, 15 (right), 17 (left), 17 (right), 20, 21, 25 (bottom), 26, 29, 30, 32, 33, 36, 38, 43 (bottom), 44 (left), 44 (right); Library of Congress, 7, 8, 9, 10, 15 (left), 18, 25 (top), 31, 34, 39 (left), 39 (right), 40 (left), 40 (right), 42 (top), 42 (second from top), 42 (second from bottom), 42 (bottom), 43 (top), 43 (second from top), 45; North Wind Picture Archives, 11; Photolibrary, 23; Red Line Editorial, 47

Edited by Jill Sherman

Cover design by Nicola Stratford, bdpublishing.com

Interior Layout by Tara Raymo

Library of Congress PCN Data

Marsico, Katie

Slavery A Chapter in American History / Katie Marsico

ISBN 978-1-62169-832-6 (hard cover)

ISBN 978-1-62169-727-5 (soft cover)

ISBN 978-1-62169-936-1 (e-Book)

Library of Congress Control Number: 2013936378

Also Available as:

Rourke Educational Media

Printed in the United States of America,

North Mankato, Minnesota

Educational Media

rourkeeducationalmedia.com

customerservice@rourkeeducationalmedia.com • PO Box 643328 Vero Beach, Florida 32964

TABLE OF CONTENTS

Chapter 1
SOLD AT AUCTION

Visitors from across the South swarmed to Savannah, Georgia in early March 1859. Hundreds of guests booked rooms at local hotels. Then they headed to a racecourse outside the city. The event that drew such huge crowds was an auction where 436 slaves were being sold.

The auction began on March 3. Buyers inspected the slaves the same way they might check a horse. The buyers pried open the slaves' mouths to check their teeth, pinched their muscles, and made them walk around. Auctioneers only cared about making as much money as possible. Sometimes they sold husbands, wives, and their children together. However, there were no promises that this would happen. Families were often ripped apart.

How did the enslaved men and women feel? How did they react to being inspected by strangers? They had to obey the white buyers and sellers. Auctioneers could not sell someone who appeared rowdy or disobedient. They were quick to whip anyone who seemed rebellious.

Slaves were treated as property and sold at auctions.

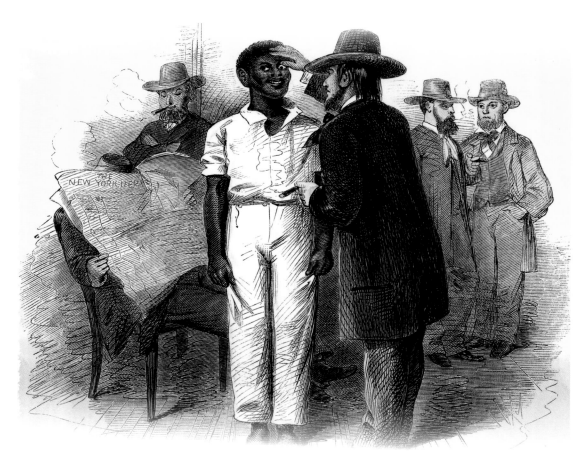

Whips were not always needed. Many of the 436 individuals wanted to impress future owners. They hoped their new owners would treat them with kindness. They desperately wished that their families would not be split apart. However, they had no control over their futures. The slaves only knew that they would always be treated as property.

THE WEEPING TIME

The slave auction in Savannah in March 1859 was one of the largest in U.S. history. It has been called the Weeping Time. The auction tore hundreds of slave families apart.

In the 1800s and earlier there were many debates about slavery in the United States. Slavery was important to the nation's economy. This was especially true in the South. There, slaves worked on cotton and tobacco **plantations**. Northern factories made cloth from cotton grown by slaves. Slavery was a huge part of the culture in some places. There had been slaves in the colonies since the 1600s. However, some people believed that slavery was wrong. They believed that one person should not own another.

This receipt is for a male slave sold for $250 in 1840.

The southern economy relied heavily on cotton and slave labor. Most slaves worked long hours, lived in poor conditions, and were not paid for their work.

The issue had grown more complicated by the time the Civil War began in 1861. Some people argued that owning another human being and treating that person as property was cruel. Unfortunately, many slave owners did not consider nonwhites to be human beings.

CRUELTY FOR MONEY

A fit, able-bodied male slave in his twenties was worth $1,600 in the 1850s. This is more than $35,000 in today's dollars. The March 1859 auction brought in $303,850, which would be more than $6 million today.

Throughout the 1800s, the nation debated whether slavery was right. This image appeared with many antislavery writings.

AM I NOT A MAN AND A BROTHER?

Some believed that slavery was good for Africans because it taught them about Christianity and Western civilization. Some slave owners did not view themselves as cruel or greedy. Some treated their slaves kindly, similar to family members. Nonetheless, slaves under the kindest masters were still not free.

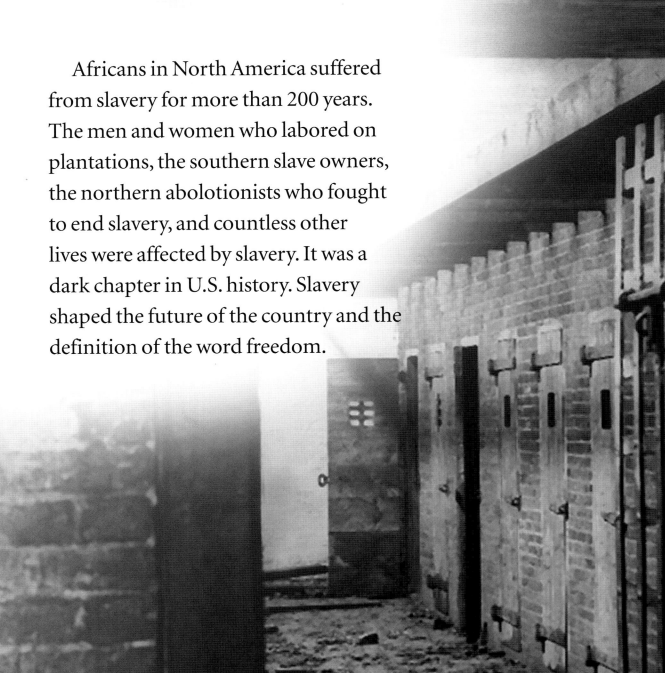

Africans in North America suffered from slavery for more than 200 years. The men and women who labored on plantations, the southern slave owners, the northern abolotionists who fought to end slavery, and countless other lives were affected by slavery. It was a dark chapter in U.S. history. Slavery shaped the future of the country and the definition of the word freedom.

Many slaves were kept in cells before they were sold.

Slaves were often transported overland, either for sale or to the property of their buyer, chained together in long lines called slave coffles.

"The expression on the faces of all who stepped on the block was always the same and told of more anguish than it is in the power of words to express. Blighted homes, crushed hopes, and broken hearts [were] the sad story to be read in all the anxious faces."
—New York Daily Tribune

Chapter 2
BEGINNINGS OF SLAVERY

Slavery is often remembered for its part in the Civil War. Yet slaves were present in North America long before the 1800s. Slavery was present on the continent as far back as the seventeenth century. At first, not all forms of forced labor involved Africans.

British colonists used **indentured servants** to work on their farms and assist in their shops. Indentured servants usually had no money to travel to the colonies. They worked for four to seven years to pay for their voyage to North America, in search of a better life. At the end of this time they became free. Some European indentured servants chose to come to North America. Others were forced to come as punishment for crimes. The first Africans in North America were indentured servants. They also became free after a certain amount of time.

Some colonists tried to enslave the native tribes for labor. These people were difficult to enslave. European diseases killed large numbers of native tribespeople. Plus, the local tribes' knowledge of the land helped them to escape.

The first Africans arrived in Jamestown in the early 1600s.

By the late 1600s British colonists needed more laborers. There were not enough people to do all the jobs in the growing colonies. Colonists began bringing more captured people from Africa. The Atlantic slave trade brought between 600,000 and 650,000 Africans to the 13 British colonies from 1700 to 1775.

A slave dealer marches captured Africans to the coast where they will be sold.

THE TRIANGULAR TRADE

The cycle of trade between Europe, Africa, and the Americas is known as the triangular trade. First, Europeans traded manufactured goods in exchange for enslaved people in Africa. After surviving the voyage the enslaved Africans were sold for sugar, tobacco, and cotton in the Americas. Finally, traders took those products back to Europe, where the cycle started over again.

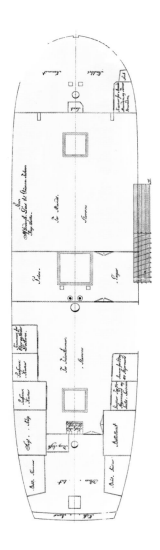

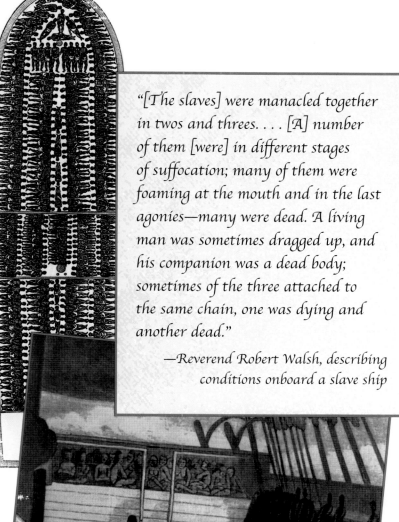

"[The slaves] were manacled together in twos and threes. . . . [A] number of them [were] in different stages of suffocation; many of them were foaming at the mouth and in the last agonies—many were dead. A living man was sometimes dragged up, and his companion was a dead body; sometimes of the three attached to the same chain, one was dying and another dead."

—Reverend Robert Walsh, describing conditions onboard a slave ship

African captives were shackled and chained, like sardines in a can, to gain maximum cargo capacity.

The majority of enslaved Africans came from west and west-central Africa. Some were captured during wars. Others were sold into slavery because they committed crimes or owed money. European buyers bought captives from African sellers. Then the buyers shipped their captives across the Atlantic Ocean.

Africans faced terrible conditions as they crossed the Atlantic Ocean. The voyage is now called the Middle Passage. Their journey was filled with disease, brutality, and death. African captives were often chained to one another. Sometimes they were chained for the entire trip. The journey could take several months.

Starvation, disease, and infection killed countless people crossing the Middle Passage. Illnesses such as scurvy, dysentery, malaria, mumps, and measles were common. Between 11 and 16 percent of the captives died at sea.

THE MIDDLE PASSAGE

A huge number of Africans went through the Middle Passage during the Atlantic slave trade. Between nine and twelve million people were taken from Africa. Between one and two million of these died at sea. Only 4 to 5 percent of all slaves landed in North America. Most slaves were taken to Central America, the Caribbean, and South America.

Indentured servants were fed and housed during their time as servants. When their contracts were fullfilled, they gained their freedom and were awarded land and supplies.

This advertisement announces the selling of slaves in Charleston, South Carolina in 1744.

> **TO BE SOLD by William** Yeomans, (in Charles Town Merchant,) a parcel of good Plantation Slaves. Encouragement will be given by taking Rice in Payment, or any leg saddles and Furniture, and Boston Rum, also and Limejuice, as well as a parcel of extraordinary Indian trading Goods, and many of other sorts suitable for the Season. Time Credit, Security to be given if required There's likewise to be sold, very good Troop choice Barbados Cordial Waters

The Africans who arrived in the Americas entered a frightening new life. They would face backbreaking work, foreigners with strange languages and customs, and a lifetime without freedom.

Chapter 3
THE NATION IN A CHANGING TIME

Eventually there were slaves in all of the British colonies. At first, imported Africans were similar to indentured servants. After working for a fixed number of years they were set free. However, as the colonies grew, the owners started losing money. Farmers and tradesmen needed a steady source of cheap labor. It was expensive to free experienced workers and train new ones.

Starting in the mid-1600s colonists wrote a series of slave codes. These laws defined slavery and took away the rights of slaves. The codes said that all slaves and children of enslaved women were enslaved for life.

Each colony had its own set of slave codes. Some codes were harsher than others. Slavery did not play the same role in every area. In the 1700s slaves were especially important in the southern colonies of Maryland, Virginia, North Carolina, South Carolina, and Georgia. In these colonies plantation owners needed many workers to grow crops such as rice and tobacco.

Slaves could be bought, sold, or given away as gifts. Their families were torn apart and their owners provided them with little food, clothing, and shelter.

Field slaves worked from sunrise to sunset, but during harvest, they worked eighteen-hour days. Slaves had to harvest, gather, and clean the cotton.

AS IF A MURDER NEVER HAPPENED

The 1705 Virginia slave codes gave white owners the right to punish their human property as they saw fit. Even murder was allowed. "If any slave . . . shall happen to be killed in disobeying, it shall not be accounted felony; but the master . . . shall be free . . . of all punishment . . . as if such incident had never happened."

There were fewer slaves in the North than in the South in the eighteenth century. Northern farms did not need as many laborers. Most northern slaves were household servants or worked in shops.

Northern colonies, on the other hand, did not have the right weather to grow those crops. Instead enslaved Africans did household chores and worked in trade shops. Slavery was much less a part of northern culture than southern culture. Slaves made up only 5 percent of the population in the North by the second half of the 1700s. In the South, slaves made up 40 percent of the population.

The culture of slavery began to change during the 1700s. American-born slaves started to replace African captives. Southern farmers came to rely on slave populations born in North America. Men and women born as slaves expected a life of labor. A slave owner's wealth increased every time another enslaved child was born. Slave owners grew rich by keeping other human beings in **bondage**.

A POLITICIAN'S PERSPECTIVE ON SLAVERY

Thomas Jefferson wrote the Declaration of Independence. He served as the third president of the United States. He did not believe in equality between blacks and whites. He also owned slaves himself. However, he was concerned about the future of slavery in the United States. He hoped slavery would eventually be stopped. In the late 1700s he wrote, "Nobody wishes more . . . to see an abolition, not only of the trade, but of the condition of slavery."

Thomas Jefferson
1743–1826

Thomas Jefferson wrote the Declaration of Independence and was the third president of the United States.

"We hold these truths to be self-evident, that all men are created equal, that they are endowed by their Creator with certain unalienable rights, that among these are life, liberty and the pursuit of happiness."

—The Declaration of Independence, 1776

Colonists fought the Revolutionary War (1775–1783) to gain national liberty. They declared their independence and won freedom from Great Britain. But were early Americans ready to grant the same freedoms to their slaves?

When drafting the laws of their new nation Thomas Jefferson, George Washington, and other founding fathers debated slavery. These men were uncomfortable with the idea of Americans owning slaves.

As the United States grew, many of the nation's founders did not want slavery to spread into new territories. However, they saw no easy way to end slavery. They feared an end to slavery would hurt the southern economy. They could not imagine what to do with the freed slaves. Whites at this time did not believe blacks could ever be their equals. Jefferson and Washington themselves were slaveholders.

George Washington
1732–1799

"I can clearly foresee that nothing but the rooting out of slavery can perpetuate the existence of our union, by consolidating it in a common bond of principal."

—George Washington in conversation at Mount Vernon, 1797

They privately acknowledged that slavery went against the ideals of the Declaration of Independence and the Bill of Rights. These documents promised basic rights and equality to all people. How could those ideas hold true in a land with slavery?

In the century that followed, these questions were constantly debated. Antislavery ideas were spreading in the North, and by the 1830s **abolitionists** were working hard to end slavery throughout the country. Northern and southern opinions about slavery would continue to grow apart until the Civil War answered the question forever.

George Washington believed in the basic rights and freedoms in the Declaration of Independence and the Bill of Rights. However, he kept slaves at his plantation, Mount Vernon.

Chapter 4
OBEDIENCE BY FEAR

The late 1700s through the early 1800s was a time of many changes. The United States was a new, independent nation. Citizens were changing their feelings about slavery. Some lawmakers started pushing harder to stop slavery from spreading.

In July, 1787 Congress passed the Northwest Ordinance. This act defined the Northwest Territory, which included much of the present-day Midwest. The act explained how new states would be made. It said that slavery was banned north of the Ohio River between the Appalachian Mountains and the Mississippi River. Twenty-one years later Congress stopped the Atlantic slave trade. But ending the slave trade from Africa did not change slavery in the South. Many blacks there had been born into slavery and slave owners no longer needed to import Africans.

Most southern states supported slavery even when people started to question the system. For a short time after the Revolutionary War, southern states allowed slave owners to free their slaves if they wanted. However, southern governments soon made it more difficult for slave owners to free their slaves. Northern states, on the other hand, began to **abolish** slavery. New laws abolished slavery right away or set a date to stop slavery. Yet northern laws did nothing to help slaves in the South.

Though white masters generally did not think they were cruel, even well-treated slaves did not control their own lives. Most men and women worked in the fields. Some women and children did chores in the master's home. A slave usually worked from sunrise to sunset. Slave owners made slaves work by beating or starving them. Certain workers called overseers rode through the fields on horseback and whipped slaves who seemed slow or lazy.

RUNAWAY SLAVES

Angry white slave owners often hunted down escapees with dogs and guns. Runaways who were caught were beaten and sometimes killed. A slave might receive 200 lashes with a whip after being returned to his master.

Slaves were not allowed to marry legally. Some slave couples held a ceremony and jumped over a broomstick to announce their relationship.

Slaves had no legal rights. They were treated as property by laws, customs, and society. The law did not recognize marriages between slaves. Masters could sell their slaves as they saw fit. Slave families could be torn apart at any moment, with children and parents all sold to different owners.

Living in small, poorly constructed cabins, most slaves were forced to tolerate difficult living situations with few possessions.

Any chance for freedom was very risky. Some slaves revolted against their masters. They used weapons and force to demand liberty. In 1822, a free African-American named Denmark Vesey planned a rebellion in Charleston, South Carolina. The plan was discovered before the revolt could happen. Whites hanged Vesey and 35 people suspected of helping him. Just nine years later enslaved preacher Nat Turner led an uprising in Southampton County, Virginia. The rebellion lasted two days and killed more than 50 whites. About two months later Turner was captured and executed.

Nat Turner was captured after he led a slave revolt in 1831.

PUNISHMENT FOR REBELLION

Southern masters were furious and frightened after slave rebellions. Many became extremely distrustful of their slaves. Some took away even more of their slaves' independence. Others used worse punishments to stop any rebellion among their slaves.

"Though I was not a murderer fleeing from justice, I felt perhaps quite as miserable as such a criminal. . . . The heart of no fox or deer, with hungry hounds on his trail in full chase, could have beaten more anxiously or noisily than did mine from the time I left Baltimore till I reached Philadelphia."

—Frederick Douglass

Escaping slaves usually fled by night.

NAVIGATING WITH THE NORTH STAR

How did escaped slaves know which way to travel as they crept through unfamiliar places at night? Many looked to the North Star. This star always appears due north in the night sky. As long as runaways headed toward it they knew they were on the road to freedom.

Slaves were punished by whipping, shackling, hanging, beating, and burning. Punishment was most often meted out in response to disobedience or perceived infractions.

Many slaves tried to sneak away to Canada or one of the free states. Running away was dangerous. Legally, masters who were trying to recover their runaway slaves could not be stopped. Laws said that anyone who found a runaway had to return that person to his or her owner.

On the long and difficult journey runaways often had trouble finding food and water. They hid during the day and traveled through unfamiliar areas by night. If caught, the punishment would be severe. Of course one of the greatest sacrifices was leaving loved ones behind. Some runaways survived and resettled in Canada or one of the free states. In turn many of those free blacks worked to help others find liberty.

Harriet Tubman
1820–1913

Chapter 5

AN END

During the 1800s the South grew angrier with northerners who helped escaped slaves. Many of these abolitionists, including Harriet Tubman, served as conductors or guides along a route called the **Underground Railroad**. Tubman was a former slave and understood the horrors of slavery firsthand. She was dedicated to rescuing other enslaved people. She and her fellow conductors guided runaways to safe houses. There, people would hide the freedom seekers from slave catchers. Conductors were committed to helping slaves reach the free states or Canada. Some historians believe that tens of thousands of slaves fled to the North by traveling the Underground Railroad.

By 1830 northern states were also known for their abolitionist journalists and public speakers. William Lloyd Garrison, a white man, published a newspaper called *The Liberator*. Garrison made many people aware of the human suffering caused by slavery. Frederick Douglass, an author, public speaker, and former slave, spoke of his time in bondage. Douglass published several of his own newspapers and books including an autobiography of his time as a slave.

Harriet Tubman was a conductor for the Underground Railroad.

Many people in northern states did not want slavery to spread. Lawmakers in proslavery areas wanted slavery to be allowed in all new territories and states. In the **Missouri Compromise** of 1820 Congress decided that slavery would be prohibited north of a line drawn across the Louisiana Purchase. The exception to this rule was Missouri, which had recently asked to become a state. Missouri was north of the line but slavery was allowed there as part of the compromise. The result was 12 free states and 12 slave states.

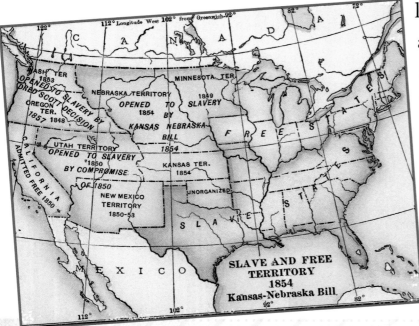

This map shows free and slave states after 1854.

THE LOUISIANA PURCHASE

In the first half of the nineteenth century many conflicts over slavery concerned the territories of the Louisiana Purchase. The United States bought this land from France in 1803. The huge area stretched from New Orleans in the South to present-day Minnesota in the North and Montana in the West. The U.S. government had to decide whether new states in these areas should allow slavery.

The decision made by Congress in 1820 did not end the conflict. During the 1850s, new laws were passed that disagreed with the Missouri Compromise. Lawmakers passed the Kansas-Nebraska Act of 1854. The act said that settlers in the Kansas and Nebraska territories could decide for themselves if they wanted to own slaves. This cancelled the Missouri Compromise and angered antislavery northerners, including future president Abraham Lincoln.

Later in the 1850s tensions increased between the North and the South. A court case involving Dred Scott made the problems worse. Scott was born into slavery in the South. His owner took him to live in Illinois and the Wisconsin Territory, both free areas. Later, Scott moved back to Missouri with his owner. When the owner died, Scott went to court for his liberty. Scott argued that his time in free areas made him a free man even if he returned to a slave state.

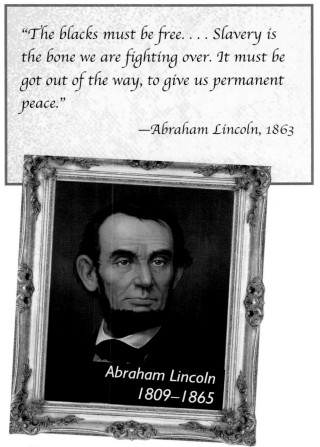

"The blacks must be free. . . . Slavery is the bone we are fighting over. It must be got out of the way, to give us permanent peace."

—Abraham Lincoln, 1863

Abraham Lincoln
1809–1865

Abraham Lincoln was president during the Civil War.

Our Country is the World, our Countrymen are all Mankind.

The Liberator *was an abolitionist newspaper founded by William Lloyd Garrison in 1831.*

Scott's case went before the U.S. Supreme Court in 1857. The judges said he had no right to file a lawsuit. They explained that blacks, whether free or slaves, were not U.S. citizens and did not have basic rights. They also declared that Congress had no power to decide whether slavery should be allowed in new U.S. territories. The issue of slavery continued to divide the country.

ONE STATE'S BLOODY BEGINNINGS

The Civil War did not start until 1861. However, there was fighting in Kansas in 1854 after the Kansas-Nebraska Act was passed. The Border War, also known as Bleeding Kansas, went on for almost four years. Proslavery and antislavery forces traded murders and raids. Each side fought to decide whether Kansas should allow slavery. In the end, Kansas became a free state in 1861.

Frederick Douglass
1817–1895

Dred Scott
1795–1858

Abraham Lincoln was famous for his antislavery views. When he was elected president in 1860 some southern states were concerned. They worried that Lincoln would try to abolish slavery. In 1861 southern states started to **secede**, or withdraw, from the United States. They wanted to decide for themselves whether slavery should be allowed in each state. In April, 1861 the Civil War began. The seceded southern states, known as the **Confederacy**, attacked a United States fort. This marked the start of the Civil War.

Black soldiers fought for the North during the Civil War.

The regimental flag and motto of the 24th Infantry Regiment, United States Colored Troops.

LET SOLDIERS IN WAR, BE CITIZENS IN PEACE

24TH REGT. U.S. COLORED TROOPS

Portrait of black Union soldier with his family.

FIGHTING FOR FREEDOM

Over the course of four years, 180,000 blacks served in the northern army. Many blacks escaped slavery and headed north to help the Union. Yet, even in the Union army, blacks were not treated the same as white troops. A number of northerners were against slavery but still held racist views. At first blacks were only given jobs such as cooking and working in camps. Later some were allowed to fight.

Lincoln's **Emancipation Proclamation** took effect in January 1863. The proclamation freed all slaves who lived in the Confederacy. However, a proslavery government controlled most of the South. Slavery would not end until the Union won the war.

By the spring of 1865 the main forces of the Confederacy surrendered to the **Union** army. Congress passed the Thirteenth Amendment the following December. This change to the U.S. Constitution abolished slavery everywhere in the nation. The Fourteenth and Fifteenth amendments were added within five years. These amendments defined U.S. citizenship and extended the right to vote to black men.

Although millions of people had been freed, it would be another century before they gained the equality and respect they deserved. During Reconstruction, the period following the Civil War, African-Americans faced poverty, violence, and discrimination. They fought for their rights well into the twentieth century. Today, the descendants of the slaves who suffered across the Middle Passage, labored endlessly in southern farm fields, and sometimes died fighting for their liberty can live with pride. Everyone can treasure the freedoms that now define the nation.

> "I looked at my hands to see if I was the same person now that I was free. There was such a glory over everything; the sun came like gold through the trees and over the fields, and I felt like I was in heaven."
>
> —Harriet Tubman

BIOGRAPHIES

Many people played important roles throughout this time period. Learn more about them in the Biographies section.

Dred Scott (1799–1858) - Scott was a slave who sued for his freedom before the Civil War. He claimed that he was free because he had lived in a free state. The Supreme Court said blacks had no legal rights, so he could not sue. The children of his original master granted him his freedom in May, 1857.

Nat Turner (1800–1831) - Nat Turner was a slave preacher in Southampton County, Virginia. In the summer of 1831 he and approximately 60 to 70 other slaves began a two-day revolt. They murdered more than 50 whites. Turner was captured two months later and hanged with 35 others.

William Lloyd Garrison (1805–1879) - Garrison was a famous white northern abolitionist. He published the antislavery newspaper *The Liberator*. He also helped found the New England Antislavery Society and the American Antislavery Society.

Thomas Jefferson (1809–1865) - Jefferson was the third president of the United States. He was the main author of the Declaration of Independence. He owned slaves and did not believe that whites and blacks were equal. Yet he hoped that some day the United States would end slavery. As president, Jefferson outlawed U.S. involvement in the Atlantic slave trade starting in 1808.

Abraham Lincoln (1809–1865) - Lincoln was the sixteenth president of the United States. He served from 1861 to 1865 during the Civil War. A quiet, honest politician from Illinois, he was openly against slavery. His election prompted several southern states to secede. Lincoln signed the Emancipation Proclamation. He was assassinated shortly after the Civil War ended in 1865.

Frederick Douglass (1817–1895) - Douglass was born into slavery in Maryland but escaped to freedom. Once in the North, he became a famous antislavery speaker, author, and publisher. After the Civil War, Douglass fought for better treatment of African-Americans and women.

Harriet Tubman (1820–1913) - Tubman was born a slave in Maryland. She escaped to freedom in the late 1840s. She was one of the most famous conductors on the Underground Railroad. During the Civil War, Tubman was a nurse and a spy for the Union army. Later she worked for better rights for African-Americans and women.

August 1619
The first Africans arrive in the British colonies in North America.

1787
Congress passes the Northwest Ordinance.

1820
Congress passes the Missouri Compromise.

1854
Congress passes the Kansas-Nebraska Act.

November 1860
Abraham Lincoln is elected president.

April 1861
The Civil War officially begins when the South attacks Fort Sumter.

April 1865
The bulk of Confederate forces surrender to Union troops, ending the Civil War.

1868
The Fourteenth Amendment is officially added to the U.S. Constitution.

Late 1700s
Slaves make up 5 percent of the population in the North but 40 percent of the population in the South.

1808
Congress makes it illegal to buy slaves from Africa.

1831
Nat Turner carries out a slave rebellion in Southampton County, Virginia.

1854–1858
The Border War, or Bleeding Kansas, divides Kansas Territory.

1857
The U.S. Supreme Court dismisses the Dred Scott case.

December 1860
Southern states begin to secede from the Union.

January 1, 1863
The Emancipation Proclamation goes into effect.

December 1865
The Thirteenth Amendment is officially added to the U.S. Constitution.

1870
The Fifteenth Amendment is officially added to the U.S. Constitution.

REFERENCE

The Free States and Slave States

Slavery in America, 1790-1820

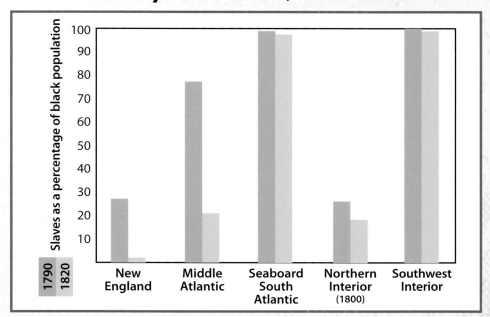

WEBSITES TO VISIT

www.pbs.org/wnet/slavery

www.besthistorysites.net/index.php/american-history/1800/south-slavery

www.history.com/topics/slavery

SHOW WHAT YOU KNOW

1. Describe a slave auction. How did the slaves feel?

2. What were the abolitionists working for in America?

3. Define indentured servants. How were indentured servants different than slaves?

4. How did the Northwest Ordinance affect the slave trade?

5. How did the Underground Railroad work to help slaves?

GLOSSARY

abolish (uh-BOL-ish): end officially

abolitionists (ab-uh-LISH-uh-nists): men and women who worked to end slavery

bondage (BON-dij): slavery

Confederacy (kuhk-FED-ur-uh-see): the states that seceded from the United States; the South

Emancipation Proclamation (i-MAN-si-pay-shun prok-la-MAY-shun): Lincoln's order that freed slaves in the Confederacy

indentured servants (in-DEN-churd SUR-vuhnts): laborers who work for a set period of time

Missouri Compromise (mi-ZUR-ee KOM-pruh-mize): an 1820 agreement intended to prevent fighting over slavery

plantations (plan-TAY-shuhns): large farms that need many workers

secede (si-SEED): to withdraw from a group or organization

Underground Railroad (UHN-der-ground RAYL-rohd): secret networks that helped slaves to freedom before the Civil War

Union (YOON-yuhn): the states that did not secede from the United States; the North

INDEX